GREATEST
Sports Stars

by Matt Doeden

CAPSTONE PRESS
a capstone imprint

Sports Illustrated KIDS

GREATEST Sports Stars

by Matt Doeden

Table of Contents

Go For It!

Whoosh! Tom Brady chucks a deep bomb down the field. Crack! Ryan Howard smashes a home run over the fence. Thump! Cristiano Ronaldo makes a diving block to save the score. No matter what sport they play, the world's greatest athletes give it their all on game day. Fans love watching powerful slap shots, high-flying snowboard stunts, and huge slam dunks. They go wild when their favorite sports stars make huge plays to win the day!

pinpoint **passes**   big-time **batting**

intense **action**

solid **defense**

baseball

basketball

football

boxing

soccer

8

hockey

snowboarding

stock car racing

swimming

tennis

track and field

Name: Carmelo Kiyan Anthony
Born: May 29, 1984, in
       New York City, New York
College: Syracuse University
Height: 6 feet, 8 inches
Weight: 230 pounds
Position: Forward

Regular Season Stats

Year	Team	Games	PPG	RPG	APG	SPG
2003–2004	DEN	82	21.0	6.1	2.8	1.2
2004–2005	DEN	75	20.8	5.7	2.6	0.9
2005–2006	DEN	80	26.5	4.9	2.7	1.1
2006–2007	DEN	65	28.9	6.0	3.8	1.2
2007–2008	DEN	77	25.7	7.4	3.4	1.3
2008–2009	DEN	66	22.8	6.8	3.4	1.1
CAREER		**445**	**24.3**	**6.2**	**3.1**	**1.1**

(PPG = points per game; RPG = rebounds per game;
APG = assists per game; SPG = steals per game)

achievements

All-Star selection: 2008, 2009, 2010
NBA All-Rookie First Team: 2004
NCAA Final Four Most Outstanding
       Player: 2003
Big East Conference Freshman of the
       Year: 2003
Olympic Gold Medalist: 2008

fact

Anthony played just one season of college
basketball. In 2002–2003, he led Syracuse
University to the NCAA championship.

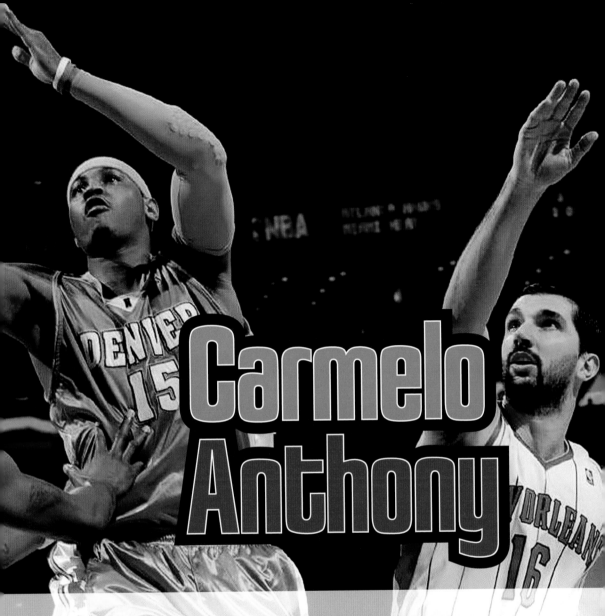

Carmelo Anthony

Denver Nuggets forward Carmelo Anthony can score from anywhere on the basketball court. He can drive the ball inside or pop a jump shot from outside. His smooth style and shooting ability have made him one of the National Basketball Association's (NBA's) best scorers. He was also a force in helping Team USA win the gold medal at the 2008 Olympic Games.

Usain Bolt

Usain Bolt is the fastest man in the world. He holds world records in the 100-meter dash, 200-meter dash, and 4x100-meter relay. He also won gold in all three events at the 2008 Olympic Games. The sprinter from Jamaica has earned the nickname "Lightning Bolt" for his blazing speed.

Name: Usain St. Leo Bolt
Born: August 21, 1986, in
Sherwood Content, Trelawny, Jamaica
Height: 6 feet 5 inches   Weight: 190 pounds

career stats

Olympics

Year	Gold	Silver	Bronze
2004	0	0	0
2008	3	0	0
Career	3	0	0

World Championships

Year	Gold	Silver	Bronze
2007	0	2	0
2009	3	0	0
Career	3	2	0

achievements

Set a world-record time of 9.58 in the
100-meter dash in 2009
Set a world-record time of 19.19 in the
200-meter dash in 2009
Laureus World Sportsman of the Year: 2009
Won gold in the 200-meter dash at the
2002 World Junior Championships

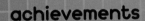

fact | As a child, Bolt had little interest in track.
His favorite sports were soccer and cricket.

Name: Thomas Edward Brady Jr.
Born: August 3, 1977, in San Mateo, California
College: University of Michigan
Height: 6 feet 4 inches
Weight: 225 pounds
Position: Quarterback

Regular Season Passing Stats

Year	Team	Games	Att.	Comp.	Yards	TD	Int.
2000	NE	1	3	1	6	0	0
2001	NE	15	413	264	2,843	18	12
2002	NE	16	601	373	3,764	28	14
2003	NE	16	527	317	3,620	23	12
2004	NE	16	474	288	3,692	28	14
2005	NE	16	530	334	4,110	26	14
2006	NE	16	516	319	3,529	24	12
2007	NE	16	578	398	4,806	50	8
2008	NE	1	11	7	76	0	0
2009	NE	16	565	371	4,398	28	13
CAREER		**129**	**4,218**	**2,672**	**30,844**	**225**	**99**

(Att. = passing attempts; Comp. = completions;
TD = passing touchdowns; Int. = interceptions)

achievements

Pro Bowl selection: 2001, 2004, 2005, 2007, 2009
NFL Most Valuable Player: 2007
Super Bowl champion: 2001, 2003, 2004
Super Bowl MVP: 2001, 2003
NFL record 50 touchdown passes in 2007
NFL Comeback Player of the Year: 2009

fact | In 2008, Brady hurt his knee in the first game of the season. He needed surgery and missed the rest of the year.

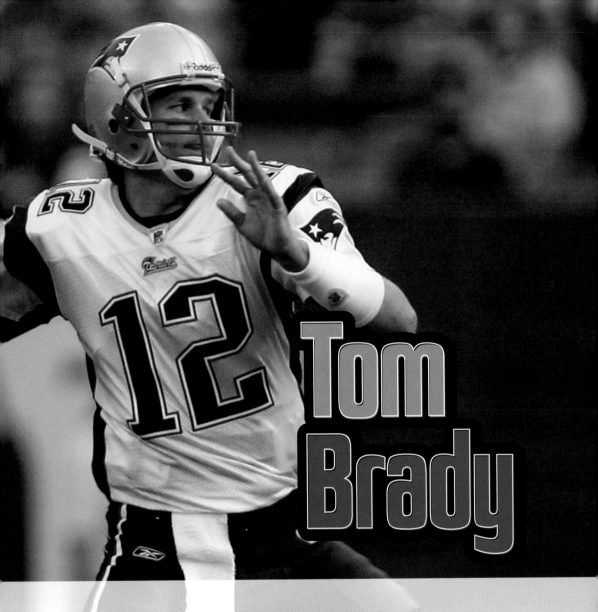

Tom Brady

Tom Brady always knows how to pick apart a defense. He can find holes in the line or hit his receivers deep. Brady barely played during his first season in the National Football League (NFL). But he really burst onto the scene in 2001. He led the New England Patriots to the Super Bowl championship. It was just the first of three Super Bowl titles. In 2007, Brady tossed an amazing record 50 touchdown passes!

Regular Season Passing Stats

Year	Team	Games	Att.	Comp.	Yards	TD	Int.
2001	SDG	1	27	15	221	1	0
2002	SDG	16	526	320	3,284	17	16
2003	SDG	11	356	205	2,108	11	15
2004	SDG	15	400	262	3,159	27	7
2005	SDG	16	500	323	3,576	24	15
2006	NOR	16	554	356	4,418	26	11
2007	NOR	16	652	440	4,423	28	18
2008	NOR	16	635	413	5,069	34	17
2009	NOR	15	514	363	4,388	34	11
CAREER		**122**	**4,164**	**2,697**	**30,646**	**202**	**110**

(Att. = passing attempts; Comp. = completions;
TD = passing touchdowns; Int. = interceptions)

achievements

Pro Bowl selection: 2004, 2006, 2008, 2009
Comeback Player of the Year: 2004
Offensive Player of the Year: 2008
Led NFL in passing yards: 2006, 2008
Big Ten Conference MVP: 2000
Super Bowl MVP: 2010

fact | In 2008, Brees passed for 300 or more yards in 10 games. He was only the second quarterback in NFL history to hit that mark.

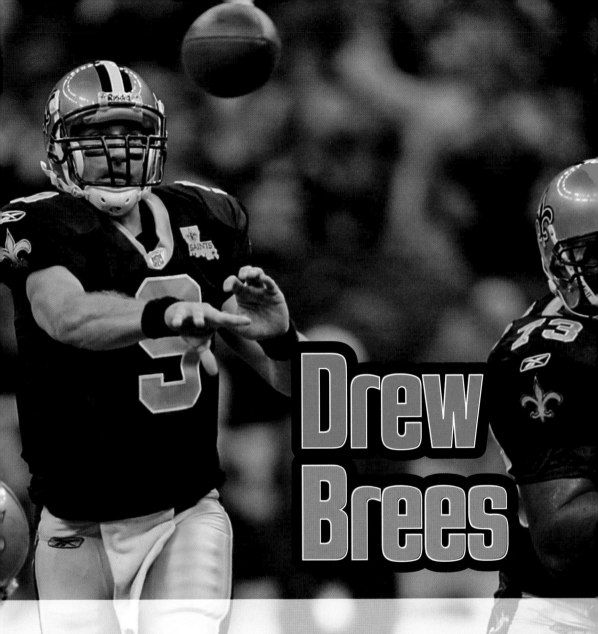

Drew Brees

Defenses often struggle to stop Drew Brees. The New Orleans Saints quarterback has a cannon for an arm. He's strong, accurate, and one of the best passers in the game. In 2008, Brees passed for 5,069 yards. It was the second highest total in NFL history. He barely missed Dan Marino's record of 5,084 yards. He led his team to win the Super Bowl in 2010.

Name: Martin Pierre Brodeur
Born: May 6, 1972, in Montreal,
    Quebec, Canada
Height: 6 feet, 2 inches
Weight: 215 pounds
Catches: Left-handed
Position: Goaltender

Regular-Season Stats

Year	Team	G	W	L	T	SO	GAA
1991–1992	NJ	4	2	1	0	0	3.35
1993–1994	NJ	47	27	11	8	3	2.40
1994–1995	NJ	40	19	11	6	3	2.45
1995–1996	NJ	77	34	30	12	6	2.34
1996–1997	NJ	67	37	14	13	10	1.88
1997–1998	NJ	70	43	17	8	10	1.89
1998–1999	NJ	70	39	21	10	4	2.29
1999–2000	NJ	72	43	20	8	6	2.24
2000–2001	NJ	72	42	17	11	9	2.32
2001–2002	NJ	73	38	26	9	4	2.15
2002–2003	NJ	73	41	29	9	9	2.02
2003–2004	NJ	75	38	26	11	11	2.03
2005–2006	NJ	73	43	23	7	5	2.57
2006–2007	NJ	78	48	23	7	12	2.18
2007–2008	NJ	77	44	27	6	4	2.17
2008–2009	NJ	31	19	9	3	5	2.41
CAREER		**999**	**557**	**305**	**128**	**101**	**2.29**

(G = games; W = wins; L = losses; T = ties/overtime;
SO = shutouts; GAA = goals against average)

fact

Brodeur's great goaltending helped Canada
win the 2002 Olympic gold medal.

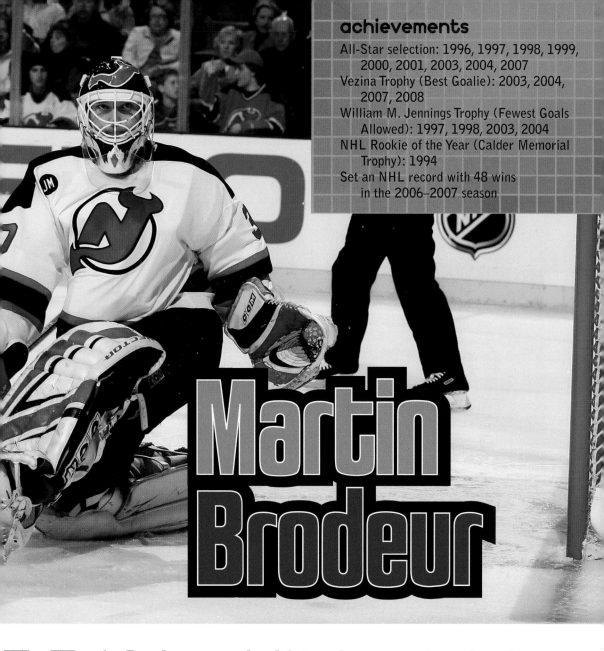

Martin Brodeur

Martin Brodeur may be history's greatest goaltender. The New Jersey Devils goalie always seems to know just where the puck is. His knowledge of the game and quick reflexes help him block many difficult shots. Brodeur is the National Hockey League's (NHL's) all-time leader in both wins and shutouts. He's won three Stanley Cups and two Olympic gold medals with Team Canada.

Kobe Bryant

Kobe Bryant thrives in the clutch. The Los Angeles Lakers guard is at his best when the game is on the line. He can shoot from the outside or drive into the lane and score inside. Bryant is a great defender too. He's been selected to the NBA's All-Defensive First Team seven times. Bryant was the 2007–2008 NBA Most Valuable Player (MVP). He is also a four-time NBA champion.

Name: Kobe Bean Bryant
Born: August 23, 1978, in
 Philadelphia, Pennsylvania
Height: 6 feet, 6 inches   Weight: 205 pounds
Position: Guard

Regular Season Stats

Year	Team	Games	PPG	RPG	APG	SPG
1996–1997	LAL	71	7.6	1.9	1.3	0.7
1997–1998	LAL	79	15.4	3.1	2.5	0.9
1998–1999	LAL	50	19.9	5.3	3.8	1.4
1999–2000	LAL	66	22.5	6.3	4.9	1.6
2000–2001	LAL	68	28.5	5.9	5.0	1.7
2001–2002	LAL	80	25.2	5.5	5.5	1.5
2002–2003	LAL	82	30.0	6.9	5.9	2.2
2003–2004	LAL	65	24.0	5.5	5.1	1.7
2004–2005	LAL	66	27.6	5.9	6.0	1.3
2005–2006	LAL	80	35.4	5.3	4.5	1.8
2006–2007	LAL	77	31.6	5.7	5.4	1.4
2007–2008	LAL	82	28.3	6.3	5.4	1.8
2008–2009	LAL	82	26.8	5.2	4.9	1.5
CAREER		**948**	**24.8**	**5.3**	**4.6**	**1.5**

(PPG = points per game; RPG = rebounds per game;
APG = assists per game; SPG = steals per game)

achievements

All-Star selection: 1998, 2000, 2001, 2002, 2003,
 2004, 2005, 2006, 2007, 2008, 2009, 2010
All-Star Game MVP: 2002, 2007, 2009
NBA MVP: 2007–2008
NBA Finals MVP: 2009
NBA All-Defensive First Team: 2000, 2003, 2004, 2006,
 2007, 2008, 2009
Averaged career-high 35.4 points per game in 2005–2006

fact — Bryant's father was Joe "Jellybean" Bryant.
He played for the Philadelphia 76ers, San
Diego Clippers, and Houston Rockets.

personal information

Name: Sidney Patrick Crosby
Born: August 7, 1987, in Cole Harbor,
    Nova Scotia, Canada
Height: 5 feet, 11 inches
Weight: 200 pounds
Shoots: Left-handed
Position: Center

Regular Season Stats

Year	Team	Games	G	A	P
2005–2006	PIT	81	39	63	102
2006–2007	PIT	79	36	83	120
2007–2008	PIT	53	24	48	72
2008–2009	PIT	77	33	70	103
CAREER		**290**	**132**	**264**	**397**

(G = goals; A = assists; P = points)

achievements

All-Star selection: 2007, 2008, 2009
NHL MVP (Hart Memorial Trophy): 2007
NHL Leading Scorer (Art Ross Trophy): 2007
NHL All-Rookie Team: 2006
Captain of Stanley Cup Championship
    Team: 2009
Led Team Canada to win gold at the
    2010 Olympics

fact

In the 2010 Winter Olympics, Crosby scored
the game-winning goal in overtime to give
Team Canada the gold medal in hockey.

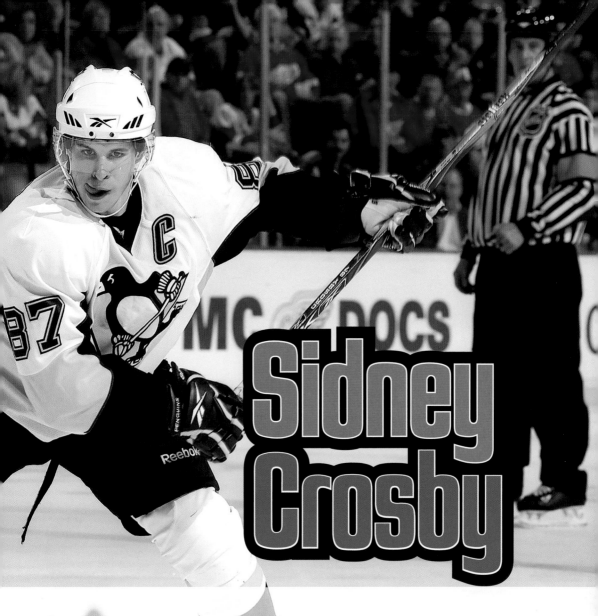

Sidney Crosby

Sidney Crosby started his NHL career at age 18. But he quickly made his mark as one of hockey's greatest players. There is little the Pittsburgh Penguins center can't do on the ice. His speedy skating, sharp passes, and lightning shots make him a constant threat to score. His skill and leadership helped the Penguins win the Stanley Cup in 2009.

Tim Duncan

Tim Duncan isn't flashy, but he's a winner. The San Antonio Spurs forward rarely shows emotion on the court. But he's a real force in the paint. Duncan is a great rebounder and inside scorer. He's one of the league's best defenders too. Duncan's skills have helped him win two MVP awards and four NBA championships.

Regular Season Stats

Year	Team	Games	PPG	RPG	APG	BPG
1997–1998	SAS	82	21.1	11.9	2.7	2.5
1998–1999	SAS	50	21.7	11.4	2.4	2.5
1999–2000	SAS	74	23.2	12.4	3.2	2.2
2000–2001	SAS	82	22.2	12.2	3.0	2.3
2001–2002	SAS	82	25.5	12.7	3.7	2.5
2002–2003	SAS	81	23.3	12.9	3.9	2.9
2003–2004	SAS	69	22.3	12.4	3.1	2.7
2004–2005	SAS	66	20.3	11.1	2.7	2.6
2005–2006	SAS	80	18.6	11.0	3.2	2.0
2006–2007	SAS	80	20.0	10.6	3.4	2.4
2007–2008	SAS	78	19.3	11.3	2.8	1.9
2008–2009	SAS	75	19.3	10.7	3.5	1.7
CAREER		**899**	**21.4**	**11.7**	**3.1**	**2.4**

(PPG = points per game; RPG = rebounds per game;
APG = assists per game; BPG = blocks per game)

achievements

All-Star selection: 1998, 2000, 2001, 2002, 2003,
2004, 2005, 2006, 2007, 2008, 2009, 2010
NBA MVP: 2002, 2003
Rookie of the Year: 1998
NBA Finals MVP: 1999, 2003, 2005
NBA champion: 1999, 2003, 2005, 2007

fact

Duncan grew up wanting to be a swimmer.
He switched to basketball after a hurricane
destroyed the only large pool near his home.

Regular-Season Stats

Year	Team	Games	PPG	RPG	APG	SPG
2007–2008	SEA	80	20.3	4.4	2.4	1.0
2008–2009	OKL	79	25.3	6.5	2.8	1.3
CAREER		**159**	**22.8**	**5.5**	**2.6**	**1.2**

(PPG = points per game; RPG = rebounds per game;
APG = assists per game; SPG = steals per game)

achievements

All-Star selection: 2010
NBA Rookie of the Year: 2008
NBA Rookie Challenge MVP: 2009
ESPN College Player of the Year: 2007
Associated Press Player of the Year: 2007

fact

Durant wears jersey number 35 in honor of
his former coach Charles Craig, who was
killed at age 35.

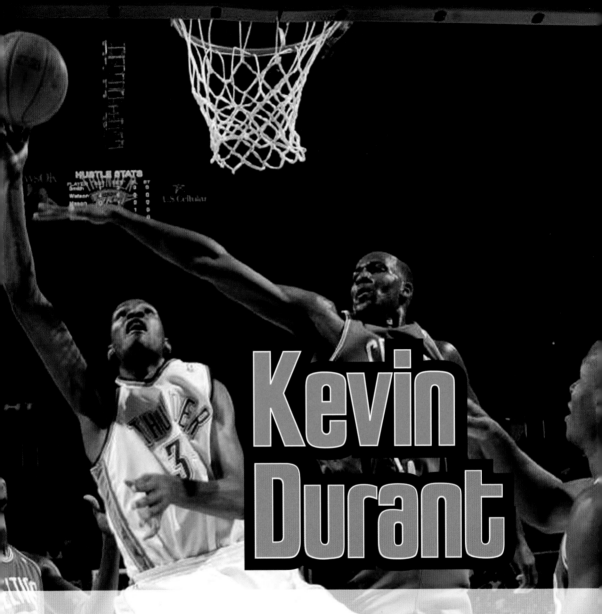

Kevin Durant

Kevin Durant is built to score. His long, lanky frame makes him a force inside. He also has a sweet touch that makes him a big threat from long distance. In 2007, he was the second overall pick of the NBA draft. The Oklahoma City Thunder forward made an immediate impact in the NBA and has been improving ever since. There's no telling how good he can be.

Roger Federer

Roger Federer may be the greatest tennis player of all time. His combination of power, accuracy, and intelligence on the court are unmatched. He's best known for his crushing forehand shot, but there's no tennis shot he can't make. Federer's great skill set has helped him win a record 16 Grand Slam titles. He even once held the number one ranking for a record 237 straight weeks!

Name: Roger Federer
Born: August 8, 1981, in Basel, Switzerland
Height: 6 feet, 1 inch
Weight: 177 pounds
Plays: Right-handed

career singles stats

Year	Wins	Losses	Titles	GST	Ranking
1998	2	3	0	0	301
1999	13	17	0	0	64
2000	36	29	0	0	29
2001	49	21	1	0	13
2002	58	23	3	0	6
2003	78	17	7	1	2
2004	74	6	11	3	1
2005	81	4	11	2	1
2006	92	5	12	3	1
2007	68	9	8	3	1
2008	66	15	4	1	2
2009	61	12	4	2	1
CAREER	678	161	61	16	--

(GST = Grand Slam Titles)

achievements

One of six men to complete the career Grand Slam:
  (Australian Open, French Open, Wimbledon,
  and U.S. Open)
Won Wimbledon five times in a row (2003–2007)
Owns eight career tournament titles in doubles
Has appeared in a record 21 Grand Slam finals

fact | Federer's serve has been clocked at up to 137 miles (220 kilometers) per hour!

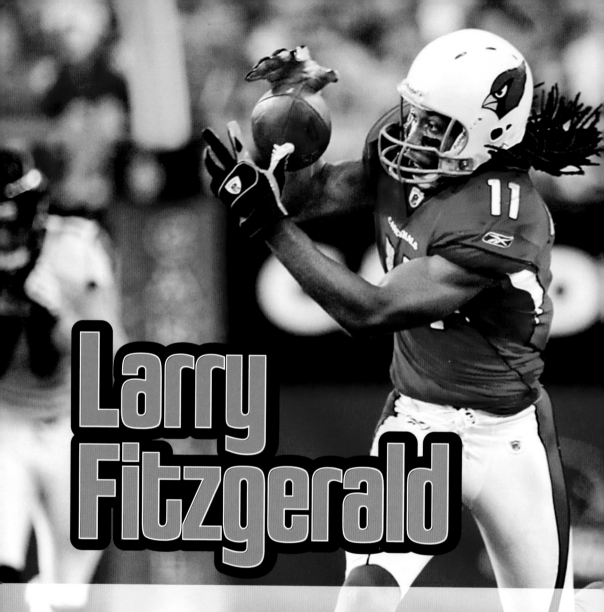

Larry Fitzgerald

Larry Fitzgerald can catch almost any pass. He is big and strong, and has great hands. He can jump higher than most defenders. In 2005, Fitzgerald led the league with 103 receptions. Fitzgerald was on fire in 2008. He grabbed a record seven touchdown catches in the playoffs. His steady hands led the Arizona Cardinals to the Super Bowl that year.

Name: Larry Darnell Fitzgerald Jr.
Born: August 31, 1983, in Minneapolis, Minnesota
College: University of Pittsburgh
Height: 6 feet, 3 inches
Weight: 217 pounds
Position: Wide Receiver

Regular Season Receiving Stats

Year	Team	Games	Catches	Yards	Avg.	TD
2004	ARI	16	58	780	13.4	8
2005	ARI	16	103	1,409	13.7	10
2006	ARI	13	69	946	13.7	6
2007	ARI	15	100	1,409	14.1	10
2008	ARI	16	96	1,431	14.9	12
2009	ARI	16	97	1,092	11.3	13
CAREER		**92**	**523**	**7,067**	**13.5**	**59**

(Avg. = average yards per catch; TD = receiving touchdowns)

achievements

Pro Bowl selection: 2005, 2007, 2008, 2009
First-Team All-Pro selection: 2008
Led NFL in catches (103) in 2005
Tied for NFL lead in touchdown catches
    (13) in 2009
Won college football's Biletnikoff Award in
    2003 as the nation's best wide receiver
Set NFL records for catches (30), yards (546),
    and touchdown catches (7) in a single
    postseason in 2009
Pro Bowl MVP: 2009

fact | As a teenager, Fitzgerald worked as a ball boy for the Minnesota Vikings.

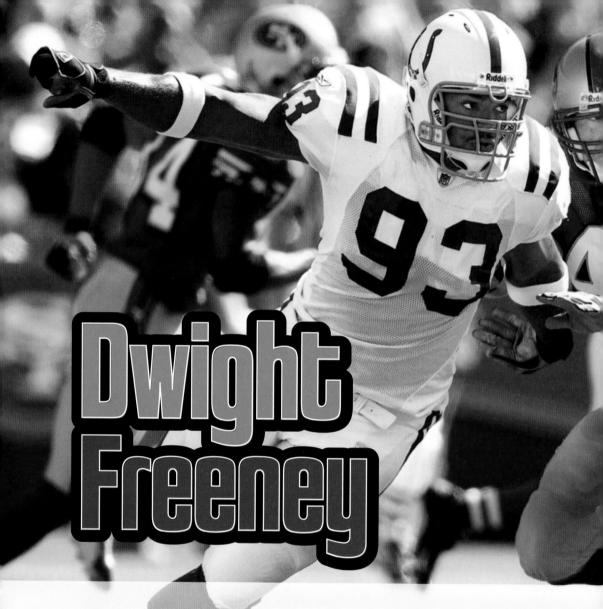

Dwight Freeney

When Dwight Freeney makes a spin move, the quarterback is in trouble. Freeney's speed-rushing style creates chaos at the line of scrimmage. As a rookie in 2002, he burst into the NFL with 13 sacks. He has been hammering quarterbacks ever since. Freeney helped the Indianapolis Colts win the Super Bowl in 2007.

Name: Dwight Jason Freeney
Born: February 19, 1980, in Hartford, Connecticut
College: Syracuse University
Height: 6 feet, 1 inch
Weight: 268 pounds
Position: Defensive End

Regular Season Defensive Stats

Year	Team	Games	Tackles	Sacks	FF	FR	TD
2002	IND	16	41	13.0	9	1	0
2003	IND	15	31	11.0	4	2	1
2004	IND	16	34	16.0	4	0	0
2005	IND	16	34	11.0	6	0	0
2006	IND	16	26	5.5	4	0	0
2007	IND	9	18	3.5	4	0	0
2008	IND	15	24	10.5	4	0	0
2009	IND	14	19	13.5	1	0	0
CAREER		**117**	**227**	**84.0**	**36**	**3**	**1**

(FF = forced fumbles; FR = fumble recoveries;
TD = defensive touchdowns)

achievements

Pro Bowl selection: 2003, 2004, 2005, 2008, 2009
First-Team All-Pro selection: 2004, 2005
Super Bowl champion: 2007
NFL sack leader (16): 2004
All-time Indianapolis Colts sack leader

fact

In high school, Freeney was an all-around great athlete. He earned letters in football, baseball, basketball, and soccer.

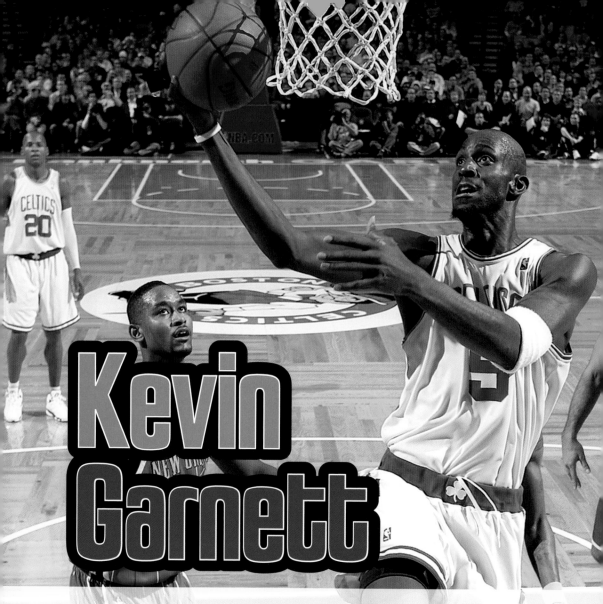

Kevin Garnett

Kevin Garnett can do almost anything on a basketball court. He can grab rebounds. He can score inside. And he has a soft shooting touch. He can also pass like a guard or defend almost any player. In 2004, "The Big Ticket" won the league MVP award with the Minnesota Timberwolves. In 2008, he led the Boston Celtics to an NBA championship.

Name: Kevin Maurice Garnett
Born: May 19, 1976, in Mauldin, South Carolina
Height: 6 feet, 11 inches
Weight: 253 pounds
Position: Forward

Regular Season Stats

Year	Team	Games	PPG	RPG	APG	BPG
1995–1996	MIN	80	10.4	6.3	1.8	1.6
1996–1997	MIN	77	17.0	8.0	3.1	2.1
1997–1998	MIN	82	18.5	9.6	4.2	1.8
1998–1999	MIN	47	20.8	10.4	4.3	1.8
1999–2000	MIN	81	22.9	11.8	5.0	1.6
2000–2001	MIN	81	22.0	11.4	5.0	1.8
2001–2002	MIN	81	21.2	12.1	5.2	1.6
2002–2003	MIN	82	23.0	13.4	6.0	1.6
2003–2004	MIN	82	24.2	13.9	5.0	2.2
2004–2005	MIN	82	22.2	13.5	5.7	1.4
2005–2006	MIN	76	21.8	12.7	4.1	1.4
2006–2007	MIN	76	22.4	12.8	4.1	1.7
2007–2008	BOS	71	18.8	9.2	3.4	1.3
2008–2009	BOS	57	15.8	8.5	2.5	1.2
CAREER		**1055**	**20.1**	**10.9**	**4.2**	**1.7**

(PPG = points per game; RPG = rebounds per game;
APG = assists per game; BPG= blocks per game)

achievements

All-Star selection: 1997, 1998, 2000, 2001, 2002,
    2003, 2004, 2005, 2006, 2007, 2008, 2009, 2010
All-Star Game MVP: 2003
NBA MVP: 2004
NBA Defensive Player of the Year: 2008
NBA champion: 2008

fact

Garnett averaged at least 20 points,
10 rebounds, and five assists per game
for a record six straight seasons.

Vladimir Guerrero

It's tough to get a pitch past Vladimir Guerrero. The Los Angeles Angels outfielder is one of the best hitters in baseball. He can hit pitches in the strike zone or out of it. Guerrero started his Major League Baseball (MLB) career with the Montreal Expos. He joined the Angels in 2004. He won the American League MVP Award that same year. Guerrero has also been an eight-time All-Star.

Name: Vladimir Alvino Guerrero
Born: February 9, 1975, in Nizao Bani,
    Dominican Republic
Height: 6 feet, 3 inches
Weight: 235 pounds
Bats: Right   Throws: Right   Position: Outfield

Regular Season Stats

Year	Team	Games	Hits	HR	RBI	AVG
1996	MON	9	5	1	1	.185
1997	MON	90	98	11	40	.302
1998	MON	159	202	38	109	.324
1999	MON	160	193	42	131	.316
2000	MON	154	197	44	123	.345
2001	MON	159	184	34	108	.307
2002	MON	161	206	39	111	.336
2003	MON	112	130	25	79	.330
2004	ANA	156	206	39	126	.337
2005	LAA	141	165	32	108	.317
2006	LAA	156	200	33	116	.329
2007	LAA	150	186	27	125	.324
2008	LAA	143	164	27	91	.303
2009	LAA	100	113	15	50	.295
CAREER		1,850	2,249	407	1,318	.321

(HR = home runs; RBI = runs batted in; AVG = batting average)

achievements

All-Star selection: 1999, 2000, 2001, 2002, 2004,
    2005, 2006, 2007
American League MVP: 2004
Silver Slugger Award: 1999, 2000, 2002, 2004,
    2005, 2006, 2007
Home Run Derby champion: 2007
National League home run leader (44): 2000

fact

Guerrero doesn't like to use batting gloves. He
says his hands are tough because as a boy he
pulled cows home with his bare hands.

James Harrison

James Harrison had to earn his playing time. He wasn't even drafted out of college. But the Pittsburgh Steelers' linebacker really shines in big games. In the 2009 Super Bowl, he intercepted a pass at the goal line. He ran it back 100 yards for the longest touchdown in Super Bowl history. Harrison was named the NFL's Defensive Player of the Year in 2008.

Regular Season Defensive Stats

Year	Team	Games	Tackles	Sacks	Int.	FF	TD
2002	PIT	1	0	0.0	0	0	0
2004	PIT	16	36	1.0	0	0	1
2005	PIT	16	36	3.0	1	0	0
2006	PIT	11	14	0.0	0	0	0
2007	PIT	16	76	8.5	1	7	0
2008	PIT	15	67	16.0	1	7	0
2009	PIT	16	60	10.0	0	5	0
CAREER		91	289	38.5	3	19	1

(Int. = interceptions; FF = forced fumbles;
TD = defensive touchdowns)

achievements

Pro Bowl selection: 2007, 2008, 2009
NFL Defensive Player of the Year: 2008
First-team All-Pro: 2008
Super Bowl champion: 2006, 2009
Holds Super Bowl record for longest play with a
   100-yard touchdown

fact

Harrison played mostly on special teams early in his career. He didn't become a full-time starter until 2007.

Matt Holliday

When Matt Holliday steps up to the plate, everyone takes notice. The St. Louis Cardinals outfielder bats for a high average and great power. He's also a threat to steal anytime he's on base. In 2007, Holliday helped lead the Colorado Rockies to the World Series. In 2009, he played for the Oakland Athletics before being traded to St. Louis.

Name: Matthew Thomas Holliday
Born: January 15, 1980, in Stillwater, Oklahoma
Height: 6 feet, 4 inches
Weight: 235 pounds
Bats: Right   Throws: Right   Position: Outfield

Regular Season Stats

Year	Team	Games	Hits	HR	RBI	AVG
2004	COL	121	116	14	57	.290
2005	COL	125	147	19	87	.307
2006	COL	155	196	34	114	.326
2007	COL	158	216	36	137	.340
2008	COL	139	173	25	88	.321
2009	OAK/STL	156	182	24	109	.313
CAREER		**854**	**1,030**	**152**	**592**	**.318**

(HR = home runs; RBI = runs batted in; AVG = batting average)

achievements

All-Star selection: 2006, 2007, 2008
Silver Slugger Award: 2006, 2007, 2008
National League batting champion: 2007
2007 National League Championship
    Series MVP
Baseball America All-Rookie Team: 2004

fact

Holliday played quarterback in high school.
He was offered a scholarship to play
football for Oklahoma State University.

Dwight Howard

Dwight Howard is a beast in the paint. Nobody works harder to block the ball and grab rebounds. The Orlando Magic made him the top pick of the 2004 NBA Draft. He is one of the NBA's best rebounders. Howard knows how to put up points too. Put it all together and he's possibly the best young "big man" in the NBA.

Name: Dwight David Howard
Born: December 8, 1985, in Atlanta, Georgia
Height: 6 feet, 11 inches
Weight: 240 pounds
Position: Center

Regular Season Stats

Year	Team	Games	PPG	RPG	APG	BPG
2004–2005	ORL	82	12.0	10.0	0.9	1.7
2005–2006	ORL	82	15.8	12.5	1.5	1.4
2006–2007	ORL	82	17.6	12.3	1.9	1.9
2007–2008	ORL	82	20.7	14.2	1.3	2.1
2008–2009	ORL	79	20.6	13.8	1.4	2.9
CAREER		**407**	**17.3**	**12.6**	**1.4**	**2.0**

(PPG = points per game; RPG = rebounds per game;
APG = assists per game; BPG = blocks per game)

achievements

All-Star selection: 2007, 2008, 2009, 2010
All-NBA First Team: 2008, 2009
Led NBA in total rebounds: 2006, 2007,
    2008, 2009
Youngest player in NBA history to reach
    5,000 career rebounds
Number one overall pick of 2004 NBA Draft

fact

Howard won the 2008 NBA All-Star Slam
Dunk Contest. In one of his dunks, he wore a
Superman cape. He took off from beyond the
free-throw line to make a huge slam dunk.

Ryan Howard

Ryan Howard can flat-out crush a baseball. In 2006, the young slugger smashed 58 home runs during his first full season. He also batted a .313 average. He was an easy pick for the 2006 National League MVP. Howard was even better in the 2008 World Series. He hit three homers to help the Philadelphia Phillies win the championship.

Name: Ryan James Howard
Born: November 19, 1979, in St. Louis, Missouri
Height: 6 feet, 4 inches
Weight: 260 pounds
Bats: Left   Throws: Left   Position: First Base

Regular Season Stats

Year	Team	Games	Hits	HR	RBI	AVG
2004	PHI	19	11	2	5	.282
2005	PHI	88	90	22	63	.288
2006	PHI	159	182	58	149	.313
2007	PHI	144	142	47	136	.268
2008	PHI	162	153	48	146	.251
2009	PHI	160	172	45	141	.279
CAREER		**732**	**750**	**222**	**640**	**.279**

(HR = home runs; RBI = runs batted in; AVG = batting average)

achievements

All-Star selection: 2006, 2009
National League MVP: 2006
National League Rookie of the Year: 2005
Led National League in home runs: 2006, 2008
Home Run Derby winner: 2006

fact

Howard is just one of three players to win the Rookie of the Year and MVP awards in back-to-back years.

Name: LeBron Raymone James
Born: December 30, 1984, in Akron, Ohio
Height: 6 feet, 8 inches
Weight: 250 pounds
Position: Forward

Regular Season Stats

Year	Team	Games	PPG	RPG	APG	SPG
2003–2004	CLE	79	20.9	5.5	5.9	1.6
2004–2005	CLE	80	27.2	7.4	7.2	2.2
2005–2006	CLE	79	31.4	7.0	6.6	1.6
2006–2007	CLE	78	27.3	6.7	6.0	1.6
2007–2008	CLE	75	30.0	7.9	7.2	1.8
2008–2009	CLE	81	28.4	7.6	7.2	1.7
CAREER		**472**	**27.5**	**7.0**	**6.7**	**1.8**

(PPG = points per game; RPG = rebounds per game;
APG = assists per game; SPG = steals per game)

achievements

All-Star selection: 2005, 2006, 2007,
    2008, 2009, 2010
All-Star Game MVP: 2006, 2008
NBA MVP: 2009
Rookie of the Year Award: 2004
All-NBA First Team: 2006, 2008, 2009
NBA scoring champion: 2008

fact

James has played for the U.S. Olympic basketball
team twice. In 2004, he and the U.S. team won
the bronze medal. In 2008, they won gold.

46

LeBron James

Nobody's going to stop LeBron James when he wants to score. James has a rare combination of speed and strength. He's almost impossible to guard. James was a huge star even before he was a pro. In 2003, he went straight from high school to the Cleveland Cavaliers. His soft touch and powerful style helped him become the 2009 NBA MVP.

Name: Derek Sanderson Jeter
Born: June 26, 1974, in Pequannock, New Jersey
Height: 6 feet, 3 inches
Weight: 195 pounds
Bats: Right   Throws: Right   Position: Shortstop

Regular Season Stats

Year	Team	Games	Hits	HR	RBI	AVG
1995	NYY	15	12	0	7	.250
1996	NYY	157	183	10	78	.314
1997	NYY	159	190	10	70	.291
1998	NYY	149	203	19	84	.324
1999	NYY	158	219	24	102	.349
2000	NYY	148	201	15	73	.339
2001	NYY	150	191	21	74	.311
2002	NYY	157	191	18	75	.297
2003	NYY	119	156	10	52	.324
2004	NYY	154	188	23	78	.292
2005	NYY	159	202	19	70	.309
2006	NYY	154	214	14	97	.343
2007	NYY	156	206	12	73	.322
2008	NYY	150	179	11	69	.300
2009	NYY	153	212	18	66	.334
CAREER		2,138	2,747	224	1,068	.317

(HR = home runs; RBI = runs batted in; AVG = batting average)

achievements

All-Star selection: 1998, 1999, 2000, 2001,
    2002, 2004, 2006, 2007, 2008, 2009
American League Rookie of the Year: 1996
World Series MVP: 2000
Gold Glove Award: 2004, 2005, 2006, 2009
New York Yankees Player of the Year: 1998,
    1999, 2000, 2006

fact

In 2000, Jeter won both the All-Star Game MVP
and the World Series MVP. He was the first player
ever to win both awards in the same season.

Derek Jeter

The New York Yankees' Derek Jeter is always confident. He has reason to be. Jeter is one of the game's great shortstops. Jeter has been a winner since he began his major league career. In 1996, he won the American League Rookie of the Year Award. Since then, he's been a 10-time All-Star and a five-time World Series champion.

personal information

Name: Christopher Duan Johnson
Born: September 23, 1985, in
Orlando, Florida
College: East Carolina University
Height: 5 feet, 11 inches
Weight: 195 pounds
Position: Running Back

Regular Season Rushing Stats

Year	Team	Games	Rushes	Yards	Avg.	TD
2008	TEN	15	251	1,228	4.9	9
2009	TEN	16	358	2,006	5.6	14
CAREER		**31**	**609**	**3,234**	**5.3**	**23**

(Avg. = average yards per run; TD = rushing touchdowns)

achievements

Pro Bowl selection: 2008, 2009
First-Team All Pro Selection: 2009
NFL Offensive Player of the Year: 2009
FedEx Ground Player of the Year: 2009
Led the NFL in rushing yards (2,006) in 2009
Gained an NFL-record 2,509 yards from
scrimmage in 2009

fact

Johnson ran the 40-yard dash in 4.24 seconds at the 2008 NFL Combine. It was the fastest time in the history of the event.

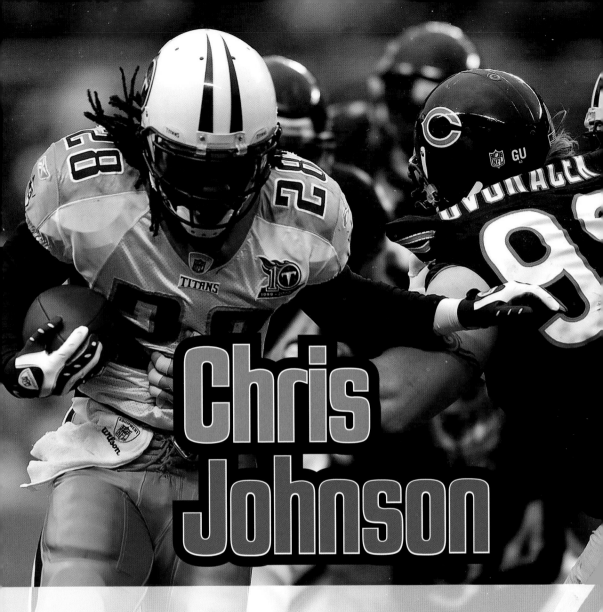

Chris Johnson

Chris Johnson terrifies defenses when he breaks into the open field. The Tennessee Titan running back may be the fastest player in the NFL. When he finds an open lane, he's off to the races. In 2009, Johnson became just the sixth running back in NFL history to rush for more than 2,000 yards. His great season earned him the NFL's Offensive Player of the Year award.

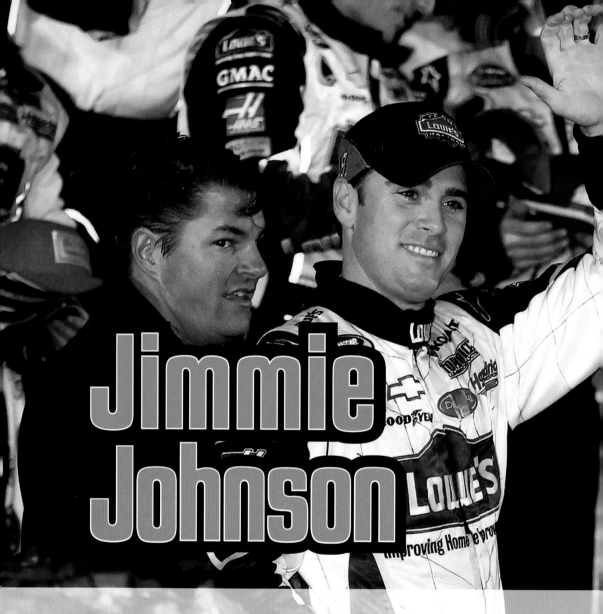

Jimmie Johnson

Jimmie Johnson is a master behind the wheel of a stock car. Johnson is known for keeping a cool head and making smart decisions on the track. Once he takes the lead in a race, he's nearly impossible to pass. And he usually knows exactly how to improve his car during a race. Johnson is the only driver in NASCAR history to win four straight championships.

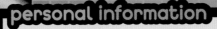

Name: Jimmie Kenneth Johnson
Born: September 17, 1975, in El Cajon, California
Height: 5 feet, 11 inches
Weight: 175 pounds
Car: #48 Chevrolet Impala

Regular Season Stats

Year	Races	Wins	Poles	T10	AVG	SF
2001	3	0	0	0	31.0	52
2002	36	3	5	21	13.5	5
2003	36	3	2	20	11.4	2
2004	36	8	3	23	12.1	2
2005	36	4	2	22	12.7	5
2006	36	5	1	24	9.7	1
2007	36	10	4	24	10.8	1
2008	36	7	11	22	10.5	1
2009	36	7	5	24	11.1	1
CAREER	291	47	33	180	13.6	--

(T10 = top-ten finishes; Avg = average finish; SF = standings finish)

achievements

Only driver in NASCAR history to win four straight
   championships (2006–2009)
Won Daytona 500: 2006
Won Brickyard 400: 2006, 2008, 2009
Associated Press Male Athlete of the Year: 2009

fact | NASCAR legend Jeff Gordon co-owns Johnson's Cup car. Gordon and Johnson are good friends and teammates at Hendrick Motorsports.

Kaká

Many people feel Kaká is the best soccer player in the world. The Brazilian midfielder, who joined Real Madrid in 2009, goes by his childhood nickname. Kaká is the total package. He's big and strong, and he's often the hardest worker on any field. Kaká has amazing ball handling and shooting skills. He sets a great example for others with his hard work and sportsmanship.

career League Statistics

Season	Team	Appearances	Goals
2001	São Paulo	27	12
2002	São Paulo	22	9
2003	São Paulo	10	2
2003–2004	AC Milan	30	10
2004–2005	AC Milan	36	7
2005–2006	AC Milan	35	14
2006–2007	AC Milan	31	8
2007–2008	AC Milan	30	15
2008–2009	AC Milan	31	16
CAREER		252	93

achievements

FIFA World Player of the Year: 2007
IAAF Latin Sportsman of the Year: 2007
"*Time 100*" most influential people: 2008, 2009
UEFA Champions League Top Scorer: 2007
Member of Brazil's 2002 World Cup-winning team

fact

At age 15, Kaká suffered a terrible spine injury in a swimming accident. Doctors feared he might never walk again. But Kaká made a full recovery.

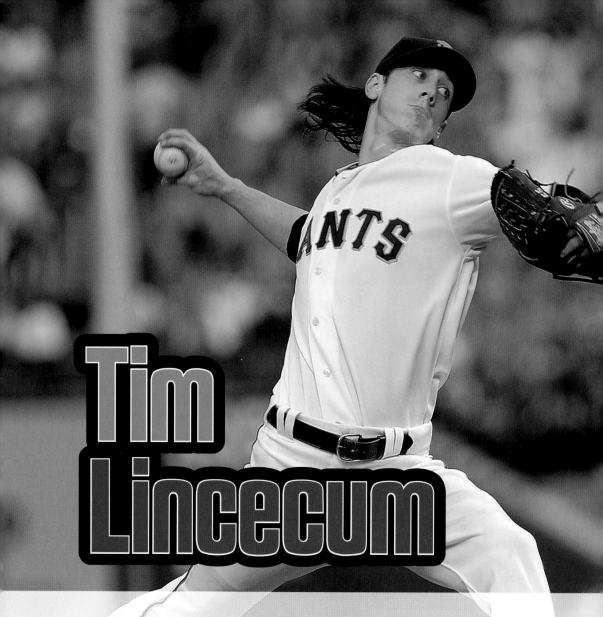

Tim Lincecum

Tim Lincecum doesn't look like a major threat on the field. The San Francisco Giants' hurler isn't as tall or heavy as most power pitchers. But his fastball clocks in at 95 miles per hour or faster. He also has a great curveball and changeup. His amazing pitching skills earned him the National League Cy Young Award in 2008 and 2009.

Name: Timothy Leroy Lincecum
Born: June 15, 1984, in Bellevue, Washington
Height: 5 feet, 11 inches
Weight: 170 pounds
Bats: Left   Throws: Right
Position: Starting Pitcher

Regular Season Stats

Year	Team	Games	Wins	Losses	Strikeouts	ERA
2007	SFG	24	7	5	150	4.00
2008	SFG	34	18	5	265	2.62
2009	SFG	32	15	7	261	2.48
CAREER		**90**	**40**	**17**	**676**	**2.90**

(ERA = earned run average)

achievements

All-Star selection: 2008, 2009
National League Cy Young Award: 2008, 2009
Led National League in strikeouts (265) in 2008
Golden Spikes Award (given to best amateur
    baseball player): 2006

fact

Despite his wild delivery, Lincecum is accurate in his throws. His father taught him the unusual pitching style to pack more power behind his pitch.

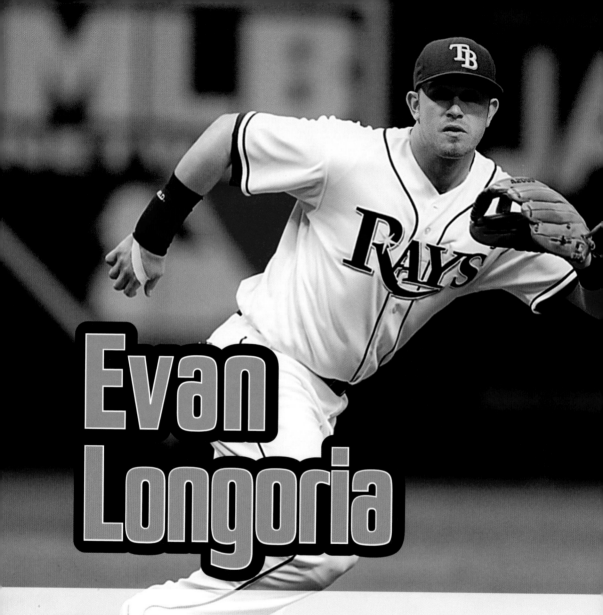

Evan Longoria

Few major leaguers hit the ball like Tampa Bay's Evan Longoria. The third baseman became an instant star in 2008. His sweet swing and great defensive skills made him the 2008 AL Rookie of the Year. He also led the underdog Rays to the playoffs that year. In his first playoff game, he hit two home runs. His great play helped the Rays reach the 2008 World Series.

personal information

Name: Evan Michael Longoria
Born: October 7, 1985, in Downey, California
Height: 6 feet, 2 inches
Weight: 210 pounds
Bats: Right   Throws: Right   Position: Third Base

Regular Season Stats

Year	Team	Games	Hits	HR	RBI	AVG
2008	TB	122	122	27	85	.272
2009	TB	157	164	33	113	.281
CAREER		**279**	**286**	**60**	**198**	**.277**

(HR = home runs; RBI = runs batted in; AVG = batting average)

achievements

All-Star selection: 2008, 2009
American League Rookie of the Year: 2008
Set Major League rookie record of four home runs
    in a playoff series in 2008
Represented the United States in the 2009
    World Baseball Classic
Gold Glove Award: 2009
Silver Slugger Award: 2009

fact | The Tampa Bay Rays made Longoria their first pick (third overall) in the 2006 draft.

59

Name: Peyton Williams Manning
Born: March 24, 1976, in New Orleans, Louisiana
College: University of Tennessee
Height: 6 feet, 5 inches
Weight: 230 pounds
Position: Quarterback

Regular Season Passing Stats

Year	Team	Games	Att.	Comp.	Yards	TD	Int.
1998	IND	16	575	326	3,739	26	28
1999	IND	16	533	331	4,135	26	15
2000	IND	16	571	357	4,413	33	15
2001	IND	16	547	343	4,131	26	23
2002	IND	16	591	392	4,200	27	19
2003	IND	16	566	379	4,267	29	10
2004	IND	16	497	336	4,557	49	10
2005	IND	16	453	305	3,747	28	10
2006	IND	16	557	362	4,397	31	9
2007	IND	16	515	337	4,040	31	14
2008	IND	16	555	371	4,002	27	12
2009	IND	16	571	393	4,500	33	16
CAREER		192	6,531	4,232	50,128	366	181

(Att. = passing attempts; Comp. = completions;
TD = passing touchdowns; Int. = interceptions)

achievements

Pro Bowl selection: 1999, 2000, 2002,
       2003, 2004, 2005, 2006, 2007, 2008, 2009
Pro Bowl MVP: 2005
NFL MVP: 2003, 2004, 2008, 2009
Super Bowl MVP: 2007
Indianapolis Colts all-time leader in
       passing yards and passing touchdowns

fact

Peyton's brother, Eli, plays quarterback for
the New York Giants. Eli led the Giants to
a Super Bowl win in 2008.

Peyton Manning

When Peyton Manning drops back to pass, defenses are in trouble. Manning has a strong arm and a great feel for the game. He can find open receivers anywhere on the field. Manning was the top pick of the 1998 NFL Draft. Since then, he's been the league's MVP four times. In 2004, Manning threw a record 49 touchdown passes. In 2007, he led the Indianapolis Colts to the Super Bowl championship.

Name: Joseph Patrick Mauer
Born: April 19, 1983, in St. Paul, Minnesota
Height: 6 feet, 5 inches
Weight: 225 pounds
Bats: Left   Throws: Right   Position: Catcher

Regular Season Stats

Year	Team	Games	Hits	HR	RBI	AVG
2004	MIN	35	33	6	17	.308
2005	MIN	131	144	9	55	.294
2006	MIN	140	181	13	84	.347
2007	MIN	109	119	7	60	.293
2008	MIN	146	176	9	85	.328
2009	MIN	137	189	28	96	.364
CAREER		**698**	**842**	**72**	**397**	**.327**

(HR = home runs; RBI = runs batted in; AVG = batting average)

achievements

All-Star selection: 2006, 2008, 2009
American League batting champion: 2006, 2008, 2009
Silver Slugger Award: 2006, 2008, 2009
Gold Glove Award: 2008, 2009
American League MVP: 2009
Number one overall pick of the 2001 amateur draft

fact

Mauer was a star quarterback and an All-American in high school. He was offered a scholarship to play football for Florida State University.

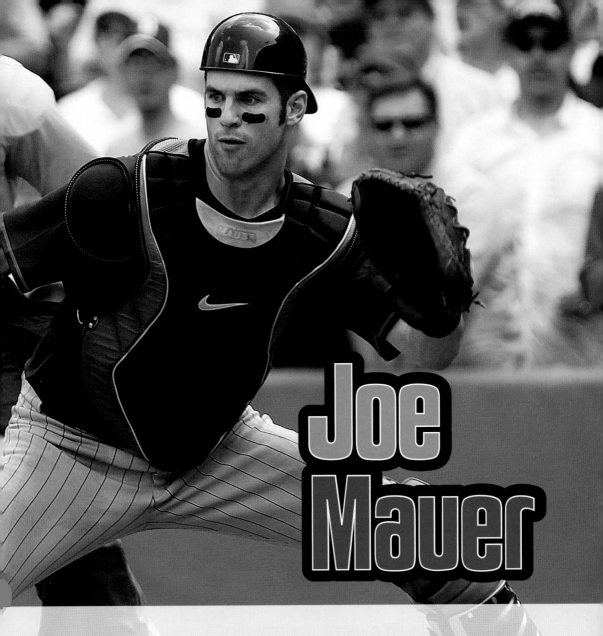

Joe Mauer

Joe Mauer's swing is a thing of beauty. Few hitters are better at waiting for just the right pitch. In 2006, the Minnesota Twins' star became the first American League catcher to win the batting title. He did it again in 2008 and 2009. Mauer is also a defensive star. Base runners think twice before trying to steal against his rocket arm. In 2009, he won the American League MVP award.

Lionel Messi

Lionel Messi's close control skills and sharp vision make him the perfect striker. Messi is one of the smallest players in the game. But the FC Barcelona star uses his small size to his advantage. He can weave through traffic like no other player. And when it looks like he's cornered, he almost always finds an opening. Only in his 20s, Messi is already one of the game's greats.

career League Statistics

Season	Team	Appearances	Goals
2004–2005	FC Barcelona	7	1
2005–2006	FC Barcelona	17	6
2006–2007	FC Barcelona	26	14
2007–2008	FC Barcelona	28	10
2008–2009	FC Barcelona	31	23
CAREER		**109**	**54**

achievements

FIFA World Player of the Year: 2009
FIFPro World Player of the Year: 2009
UEFA Club Footballer of the Year: 2009
FIFPro World Young Player of the Year:
    2006, 2007, 2008
Argentina's Player of the Year: 2005, 2007, 2009
Member of Argentina's 2008 gold medal Olympic team

fact | Messi's nickname is *El Pulga,* or "The Flea."

Name: Yao Ming
Born: September 12, 1980, in Shanghai, China
Height: 7 feet, 6 inches
Weight: 310 pounds
Position: Center

Regular Season Stats

Year	Team	Games	PPG	RPG	APG	BPG
2002–2003	HOU	82	13.5	8.2	1.7	1.8
2003–2004	HOU	82	17.5	9.0	1.5	1.9
2004–2005	HOU	80	18.3	8.4	0.8	2.0
2005–2006	HOU	57	22.3	10.2	1.5	1.6
2006–2007	HOU	48	25.0	9.4	2.0	2.0
2007–2008	HOU	55	22.0	10.8	2.3	2.0
2008–2009	HOU	77	19.7	9.9	1.8	1.9
CAREER		**481**	**19.8**	**9.3**	**1.6**	**1.9**

(PPG = points per game; RPG = rebounds per game
APG = assists per game; BPG = blocks per game)

achievements

All-Star selection: 2003, 2004, 2005, 2006,
     2007, 2008, 2009
NBA All-Rookie Team: 2003
Top overall pick of the 2002 NBA Draft
Chinese Basketball Association MVP: 2001, 2002
Chinese Basketball Association champion: 2002

fact

Yao's mother played for the Chinese women's national basketball team. His father also played for the Shanghai team in China.

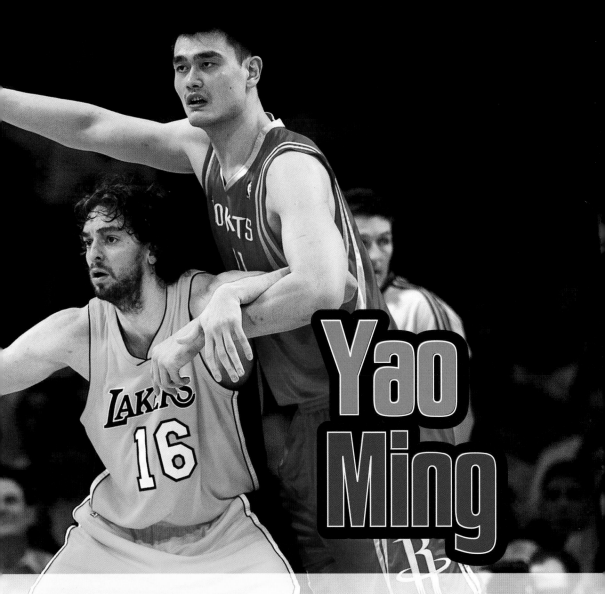

Yao Ming

Yao Ming towers over his competitors. At 7½ feet tall, he is the NBA's tallest player. He's also an international superstar. Yao was only the second player from China to join the NBA. In his home country, he led the Shanghai Sharks to a league championship in 2002. Later that year, the Houston Rockets made him the first overall pick of the draft.

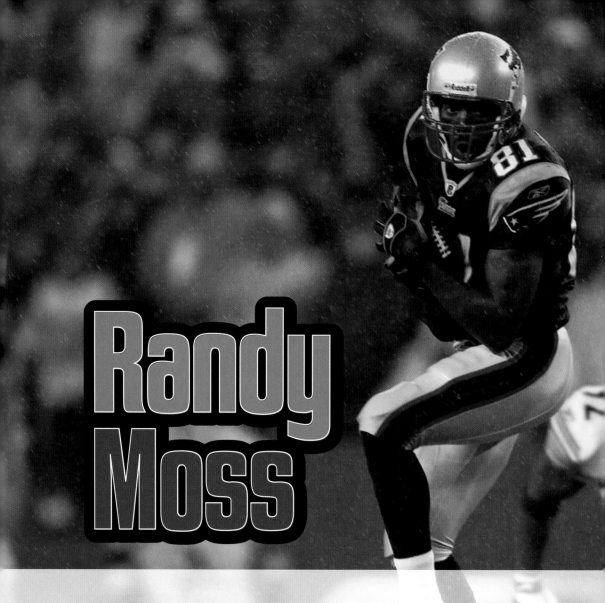

Randy Moss

Few receivers can match Randy Moss' speed, leaping ability, and steady hands. Moss lit up the NFL in 1998. He set a rookie record with 17 touchdown catches for the Minnesota Vikings. Moss has kept defenses on their toes ever since. In 2007, he set an amazing NFL record with 23 touchdown catches in a season. He helped lead the New England Patriots to an undefeated regular season.

Regular Season Receiving Stats

Year	Team	Games	Catches	Yards	Avg.	TD
1998	MIN	16	69	1,313	19.0	17
1999	MIN	16	80	1,413	17.7	11
2000	MIN	16	77	1,437	18.7	15
2001	MIN	16	82	1,233	15.0	10
2002	MIN	16	106	1,347	12.7	7
2003	MIN	16	111	1,632	14.7	17
2004	MIN	13	49	767	15.7	13
2005	OAK	16	60	1,005	16.8	8
2006	OAK	13	42	553	13.2	3
2007	NE	16	98	1,493	15.2	23
2008	NE	16	69	1,008	14.6	11
2009	NE	16	83	1,264	15.2	13
CAREER		**186**	**926**	**14,465**	**15.6**	**148**

(Avg. = average yards per catch; TD = receiving touchdowns)

achievements

Pro Bowl selection: 1998, 1999, 2000,
2002, 2003, 2007, 2009
NFL Offensive Rookie of the Year: 1998
NFL rookie record 17 touchdown catches in 1998
NFL record 23 receiving touchdowns in 2007
Pro Bowl record 212 receiving yards in 1999

fact

Moss has thrown eight passes in his NFL career. He completed four of them. Two of them went for touchdowns.

Rafael Nadal

Rafael Nadal's skills with a racquet are amazing to watch on a tennis court. His shots are powerful and accurate. His speed allows him to cover the entire court. During matches, he doesn't make many mistakes, and he doesn't wear down. His never-say-die approach has served him well. He's won six Grand Slam titles and the 2008 Olympic gold medal in men's singles.

Name: Rafael Nadal Parera
Born: June 3, 1986, in Manacor, Majorca, Spain
Height: 6 feet, 1 inch
Weight: 188 pounds
Plays: Left-handed

career singles stats

Year	Wins	Losses	Titles	GST	Ranking
2002	1	1	0	0	200
2003	14	11	0	0	49
2004	30	17	1	0	51
2005	79	10	11	1	2
2006	59	12	5	1	2
2007	70	15	6	1	2
2008	82	11	8	2	1
2009	66	14	5	1	2
CAREER	401	91	36	6	--

(GST = Grand Slam Titles)

achievements

Won a record 81 straight matches on clay surfaces
from 2005 to 2007
Won 25 tournament titles in 2005, a record for
a teenager
First player ever to win 400 or more of his first 500
singles matches
Won four consecutive French Open tournaments from
2005 to 2008

fact

Nadal is known as "The King of Clay" because
of his great success on clay courts. The slower
play on clay favors his athletic style.

Regular Season Stats

Year	Team	Games	PPG	RPG	APG	SPG
1998–1999	DAL	47	8.2	3.4	1.0	0.6
1999–2000	DAL	82	17.5	6.5	2.5	0.8
2000–2001	DAL	82	21.8	9.2	2.1	1.0
2001–2002	DAL	76	23.4	9.9	2.4	1.1
2002–2003	DAL	80	25.1	9.9	3.0	1.4
2003–2004	DAL	77	21.8	8.7	2.7	1.2
2004–2005	DAL	78	26.1	9.7	3.1	1.2
2005–2006	DAL	81	26.6	9.0	2.8	0.7
2006–2007	DAL	78	24.6	8.9	3.4	0.7
2007–2008	DAL	77	23.6	8.6	3.5	0.7
2008–2009	DAL	81	25.9	8.4	2.4	0.8
CAREER		**839**	**22.2**	**8.4**	**2.7**	**0.9**

(PPG = points per game; RPG = rebounds per game;
APG = assists per game; SPG = steals per game)

achievements

All-Star selection: 2002, 2003, 2004, 2005,
    2006, 2007, 2008, 2009, 2010
NBA MVP: 2007
All-NBA First Team: 2005, 2006, 2007, 2009
NBA Three-Point Shootout winner: 2006
Helped Germany's national team qualify for
    the 2008 Olympic Games

fact | Nowitzki had the honor of carrying
Germany's flag in the opening ceremonies
of the 2008 Olympic Games.

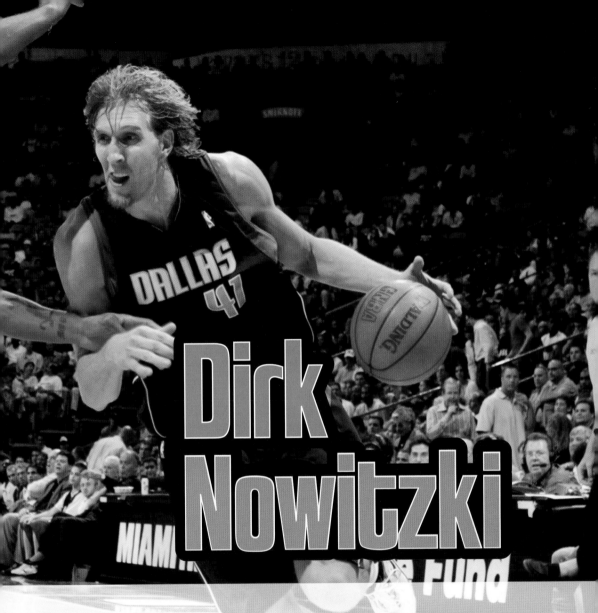

Dirk Nowitzki

Big men like Dirk Nowitzki don't usually have the skills of a shooting guard. But he handles and passes the ball with ease. And he's one of the best three-point shooters in the league. Nowitzki is also a great inside scorer and rebounder for the Dallas Mavericks. His great all-around play earned Nowitzki NBA MVP honors for the 2006–2007 season.

Name: Alexander Mikhaylovich Ovechkin
Born: September 17, 1985, in Moscow,
    USSR (Russia)
Height: 6 feet, 2 inches
Weight: 233 pounds
Shoots: Right-handed
Position: Left winger

Regular Season Stats

Year	Team	Games	G	A	P
2005–2006	WAS	81	52	54	106
2006–2007	WAS	82	46	46	92
2007–2008	WAS	82	65	47	112
2008–2009	WAS	79	56	54	110
CAREER		**324**	**219**	**201**	**420**

(G = goals; A = assists; P = points)

achievements

All-Star Game selection: 2007, 2008, 2009
NHL MVP (Hart Memorial Trophy):
    2008, 2009
NHL Leading Scorer (Art Ross Trophy):
    2008
NHL Rookie of the Year (Calder Memorial
    Trophy): 2006

fact

It's no secret that Ovechkin loves to shoot. In the 2005–2006 season, he set an NHL rookie record with 425 shots on goal. He also led the NHL in shots in each of his first four seasons.

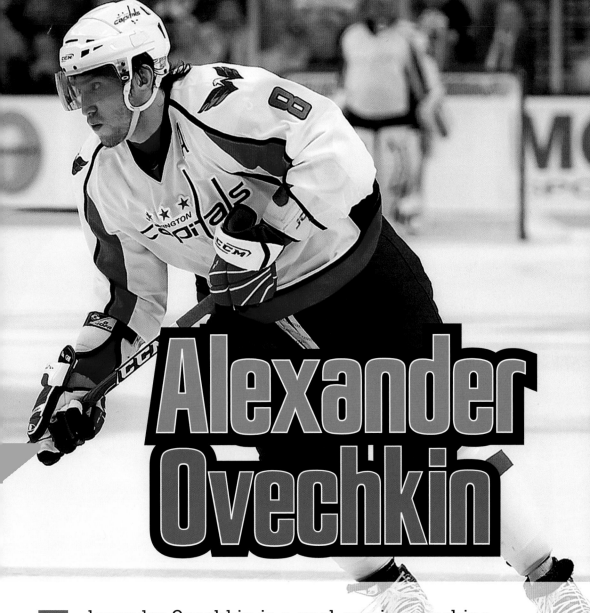

Alexander Ovechkin

Alexander Ovechkin is a goal-scoring machine. He has amazing puck control and a hard shot. Ovechkin led the NHL in scoring during the 2007-2008 and 2008-2009 seasons. He began his career in his native Russia. The Washington Capitals drafted the winger number one overall in 2004. The two-time MVP is known for his wild victory celebrations as well as his incredible skills.

75

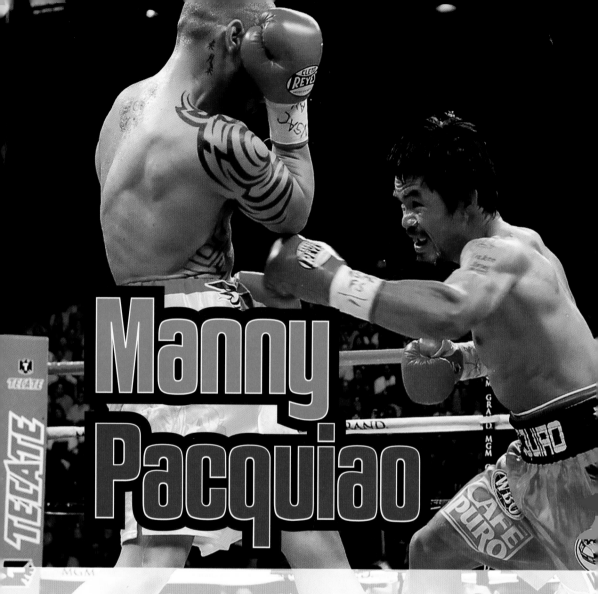

Manny Pacquiao

Manny Pacquiao isn't a big boxer, but he packs a whale of a punch. "Pac Man" has won boxing titles in seven different weight classes. That's a feat nobody else has ever matched. His speed, aggressive style, and powerful punch have made him one of the greatest boxers in the world. *The Ring* magazine ranked him the world's top fighter in 2006, 2008, and 2009.

career statistics

Year	Wins	Losses	Draws	KO
1995	10	0	0	4
1996	6	1	0	4
1997	6	0	0	5
1998	2	0	0	2
1999	3	1	0	3
2000	3	0	0	3
2001	3	0	1	3
2002	2	0	0	2
2003	3	0	0	3
2004	1	0	1	1
2005	1	1	0	1
2006	3	0	0	2
2007	2	0	0	1
2008	3	0	0	2
2009	2	0	0	2
CAREER	50	3	2	38

(KO = knockouts)

achievements

Only boxer in history to win titles in seven different
     weight classes
Named 2000–2009 Boxing Writers Association of
     America Fighter of the Decade
The Ring magazine Fighter of the Year: 2006, 2008, 2009
ESPY Best Fighter Award: 2009

fact

Pacquiao was the flag bearer for the
Philippines at the opening ceremonies
of the 2008 Summer Olympics.

Name: Christopher Emmanuel Paul
Born: May 6, 1985, in Winston-Salem,
    North Carolina
College: Wake Forest University
Height: 6 feet   Weight: 175 pounds
Position: Guard

Regular Season Stats

Year	Team	Games	PPG	RPG	APG	SPG
2005–2006	NOR	78	16.1	5.1	7.8	2.2
2006–2007	NOR	64	17.3	4.4	8.9	1.8
2007–2008	NOR	80	21.1	4.0	11.6	2.7
2008–2009	NOR	78	22.8	5.5	11.0	2.8
CAREER		**300**	**19.3**	**4.8**	**9.8**	**2.4**

(PPG = points per game; RPG = rebounds per game;
APG = assists per game; SPG = steals per game)

achievements

All-Star selection: 2008, 2009, 2010
Rookie of the Year Award: 2006
NBA assists leader: 2008, 2009
All-NBA First Team: 2008, 2009
Member of U.S. Olympic gold medal team: 2008

fact

Paul set an NBA record by making at
least one steal in 108 straight games.

Chris Paul

Nobody drives into the paint or passes like the New Orleans Hornets' Chris Paul. If a shot is open, he'll take it. If not, he'll pass the ball to an open teammate. Paul's great passing makes him one of the league's best point guards. He led the NBA in assists in the 2007–2008 and 2008–2009 seasons.

Name: Dustin Luis Pedroia
Born: August 17, 1983, in Woodland, California
Height: 5 feet, 9 inches
Weight: 180 pounds
Bats: Right   Throws: Right
Position: Second Base

Regular season stats

Year	Team	Games	Hits	HR	RBI	AVG
2006	BOS	31	17	2	7	.191
2007	BOS	139	165	8	50	.317
2008	BOS	157	213	17	83	.326
2009	BOS	154	185	15	72	.296
CAREER		481	580	42	212	.307

(HR = home runs; RBI = runs batted in; AVG = batting average)

achievements

All-Star selection: 2008, 2009
American League Rookie of the Year: 2007
American League MVP: 2008
Gold Glove Award: 2008
Silver Slugger Award: 2008

fact | In the 2007 World Series, Pedroia became the first rookie to lead off game one with a home run.

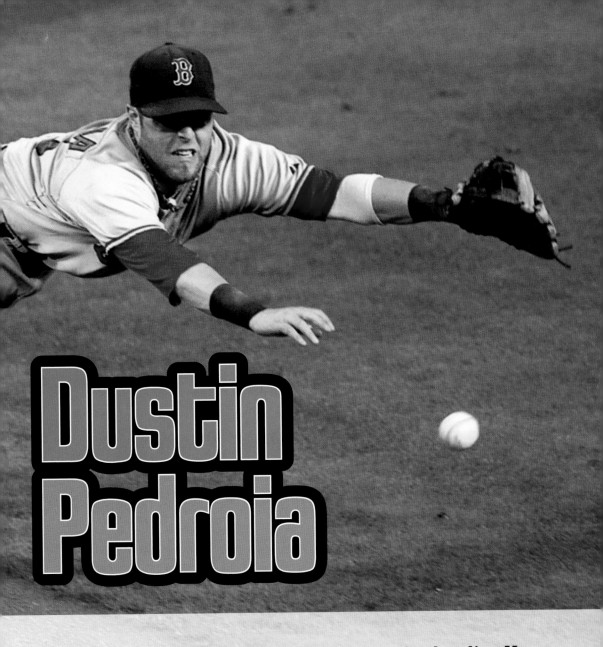

Dustin Pedroia

Dustin Pedroia spends a lot of time in the dirt. He dives all around the infield. He slides into bases at full speed. Pedroia's scrappy play helped him win the AL Rookie of the Year Award in 2007. He also helped the Boston Red Sox win the World Series that year. Then in 2008, he won the AL MVP trophy.

Name: Adrian Lewis Peterson
Born: March 21, 1985, in Palestine, Texas
College: University of Oklahoma
Height: 6 feet, 1 inch
Weight: 217 pounds
Position: Running Back

Regular Season Rushing Stats

Year	Team	Games	Rushes	Yards	Avg.	TD
2007	MIN	14	238	1,341	5.6	12
2008	MIN	16	363	1,760	4.8	10
2009	MIN	16	314	1,383	4.4	18
CAREER		**46**	**915**	**4,484**	**4.9**	**40**

(Avg. = average yards per run; TD = rushing touchdowns)

achievements

Pro Bowl selection: 2007, 2008, 2009
Pro Bowl MVP: 2008
Offensive Rookie of the Year: 2007
NFL record 296 rushing yards in a game:
    November 4, 2007, vs. San Diego Chargers
Best Breakthrough Athlete ESPY award: 2008

fact Peterson's nickname is A.D., which stands for "All Day."

Adrian Peterson

The Minnesota Vikings' Adrian Peterson is a threat to score any time he touches the ball. His speed, power, and vision are unmatched. Peterson took the NFL by storm as a rookie in 2007. In just his eighth game, Peterson set the single game rushing record with 296 yards! Peterson had an even better season in 2008. He led the NFL in rushing with 1,760 yards.

career olympic medals

Year	Events	Gold	Silver	Bronze
2000	1	0	0	0
2004	8	6	0	2
2008	8	8	0	0
CAREER	**17**	**14**	**0**	**2**

achievements

World Swimmer of the Year Award: 2003, 2004,
     2006, 2007, 2008, 2009
American Swimmer of the Year Award: 2001,
     2002, 2003, 2004, 2006, 2007, 2008, 2009
Olympic-record 14 career gold medals
Olympic-record eight gold medals in a single
     Olympic Games in 2008
Sports Illustrated Sportsman of the Year: 2008

fact

Phelps wears a size 14 shoe. His big feet
work like flippers, pushing him quickly
through the water.

Michael Phelps

With his long, powerful strokes, Michael Phelps is a natural in the water. Many believe that Phelps is the greatest swimmer of all time. This swimming sensation has won a record 14 Olympic gold medals and set 37 world records. Phelps is an expert in all strokes, but his best include the butterfly and the freestyle.

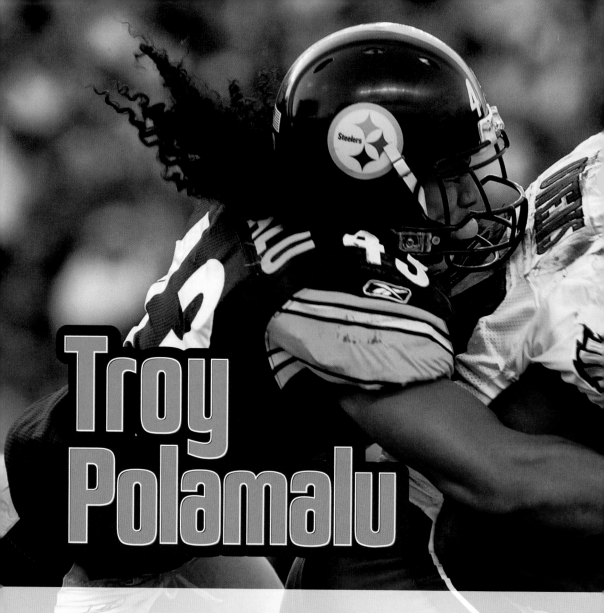

Troy Polamalu

It's hard to miss Troy Polamalu on the football field. Opposing teams are always watching for his famous long, curly hair. Polamalu's speed and strength make him one of the best defenders in the game. The Pittsburgh Steelers safety is great at containing the passing game. He's even better at blitzing the quarterback. Polamalu is a two-time Super Bowl champ and a five-time Pro Bowler.

Name: Troy Aumua Polamalu
Born: April 19, 1981, in Garden Grove, California
College: University of Southern California
Height: 5 feet, 10 inches
Weight: 207 pounds
Position: Safety

Regular Season Defensive Stats

Year	Team	Games	Tackles	Sacks	Int.	TD
2003	PIT	16	30	2.0	0	0
2004	PIT	16	67	1.0	5	1
2005	PIT	16	73	3.0	2	1
2006	PIT	13	58	1.0	3	0
2007	PIT	11	45	0.0	0	0
2008	PIT	16	54	0.0	7	0
2009	PIT	5	18	0.0	3	0
CAREER		93	345	7.0	20	2

(Int. = interceptions; TD = defensive touchdowns)

achievements

Pro Bowl selection: 2004, 2005, 2006, 2007, 2008
Super Bowl champion: 2006, 2009
NFL record three sacks in one game by a safety: 2005
University of Southern California team MVP in 2001
College All-American first team in 2001

fact

Polamalu's uncle Kennedy Pola coaches running backs for the Jacksonville Jaguars.

Albert Pujols

Albert Pujols may be the most dangerous hitter playing today. He's never finished a season with a batting average lower than .314. He's also smacked at least 32 home runs each season. The three-time National League MVP led the St. Louis Cardinals to a World Series title in 2006.

Name: José Alberto Pujols
Born: January 16, 1980, in Santo Domingo,
    Dominican Republic
Height: 6 feet 3 inches
Weight: 230 pounds
Bats: Right   Throws: Right   Position: First Base

Regular Season Stats

Year	Team	Games	Hits	HR	RBI	AVG
2001	STL	161	194	37	130	.329
2002	STL	157	185	34	127	.314
2003	STL	157	212	43	124	.359
2004	STL	154	196	46	123	.331
2005	STL	161	195	41	117	.330
2006	STL	143	177	49	137	.331
2007	STL	158	185	32	103	.327
2008	STL	148	187	37	116	.357
2009	STL	160	186	47	135	.327
CAREER		**1,399**	**1,717**	**366**	**1,112**	**.334**

(HR = home runs; RBI = runs batted in; AVG = batting average)

achievements

All-Star selection: 2001, 2003, 2004, 2005,
    2006, 2007, 2008, 2009
National League MVP: 2005, 2008, 2009
National League batting champion: 2003
National League Championship Series MVP: 2004
Gold Glove Award: 2006
Silver Slugger Award: 2004, 2008, 2009

fact | Pujols started his career as an outfielder.
He then played third base before becoming
the Cardinals' regular first baseman.

Name: Hanley Ramirez
Born: December 23, 1983, in Samana,
    Dominican Republic
Height: 6 feet, 3 inches
Weight: 225 pounds
Bats: Right   Throws: Right   Position: Shortstop

Regular Season Stats

Year	Team	Games	Hits	HR	RBI	AVG
2005	BOS	2	0	0	0	.000
2006	FLA	158	185	17	59	.292
2007	FLA	154	212	29	81	.332
2008	FLA	153	177	33	67	.301
2009	FLA	151	197	24	106	.342
CAREER		618	771	103	313	.316

(HR = home runs; RBI = runs batted in; AVG = batting average)

achievements

All-Star selection: 2008, 2009
National League Rookie of the Year: 2006
Silver Slugger Award: 2008, 2009
Florida Marlins team MVP: 2008

fact | In 2008, Ramirez led the league in scoring
with 125 runs.

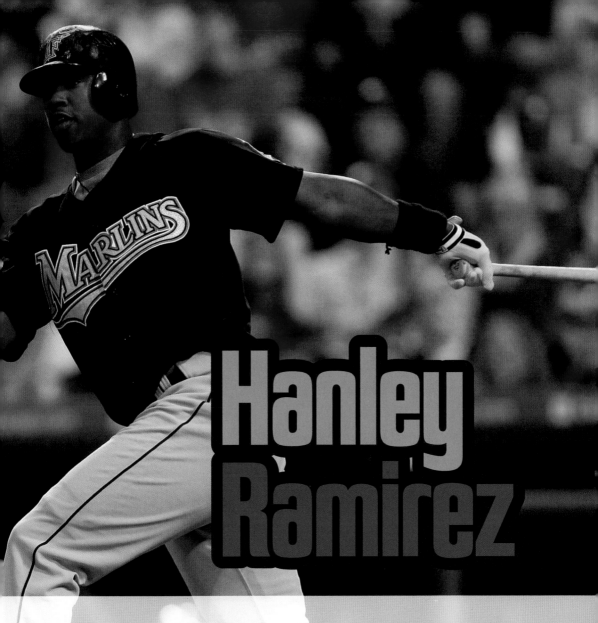

Hanley Ramirez

Hanley Ramirez is an all-around talent. He's a skilled hitter, a fast runner, and plays great defense. In 2006, he hit 17 home runs for the Florida Marlins. He also stole 51 bases. Those numbers earned him the NL Rookie of the Year Award. Ramirez has continued to get even better. He batted for a .332 average in 2007. In 2008, he smacked 33 homers.

Francisco Rodriguez

At times, the New York Mets' Francisco Rodriguez seems totally unhittable. Batters can only stand and watch as his pitches zip across the plate. Rodriguez's nickname is "K-Rod." The *K* is baseball's symbol for a strikeout. Rodriguez's best year was in 2008 with the Los Angeles Angels. He set a major league record with 62 saves.

Regular Season Stats

Year	Team	Games	Wins	Losses	ERA	Saves
2002	ANA	5	0	0	0.00	0
2003	ANA	59	8	3	3.03	2
2004	ANA	69	4	1	1.82	12
2005	LAA	66	2	5	2.67	45
2006	LAA	69	2	3	1.73	47
2007	LAA	64	5	2	2.81	40
2008	LAA	76	2	3	2.24	62
2009	NYM	70	3	6	3.71	35
CAREER		**478**	**26**	**23**	**2.53**	**243**

(ERA = earned run average)

achievements

All-Star selection: 2004, 2007, 2008, 2009
Led American League in saves: 2005, 2006, 2008
Rolaids Relief Man of the Year Award: 2006, 2008
Major league record 62 saves in 2008
World Series champion: 2002

fact

In 2006, Rodriguez saved his 100th career game at age 24. He became the youngest pitcher ever to reach that mark.

Ronaldinho

Soccer fans hold their breath when Ronaldinho finds open space on the field. They know something exciting is about to happen. AC Milan's Brazilian midfielder is one of the greatest solo attackers of all time. Ronaldinho has incredible ball control and an accurate shot. His skills have helped him become a two-time FIFA World Player of the Year.

career League statistics

Season	Team	Appearances	Goals
1998	Grêmio	6	1
1999	Grêmio	17	6
2000	Grêmio	21	14
2001–2002	Paris Saint-Germain	28	9
2002–2003	Paris Saint-Germain	27	8
2003–2004	FC Barcelona	32	15
2004–2005	FC Barcelona	35	9
2005–2006	FC Barcelona	29	17
2006–2007	FC Barcelona	32	21
2007–2008	FC Barcelona	17	8
2008–2009	AC Milan	26	8
CAREER		270	116

achievements

FIFA World Player of the Year: 2004, 2005
European Footballer of the Year: 2005
FIFPro World Player of the Year: 2005, 2006
FIFA Confederations Cup Top Scorer: 1999
Member of Brazilian Olympic bronze medal
    team: 2008
Golden Foot award: 2009

fact

Ronaldinho is Portuguese for "Little Ronaldo."
He earned the nickname because he started
playing at a very early age. In Brazil, Ronaldinho
is also known by the nickname *Gaúcho*.

Name: Cristiano Ronaldo dos Santos Aveiro
Born: February 5, 1985, in Funchal,
    Madeira, Portugal
Height: 6 feet, 1 inch
Weight: 165 pounds
Position: Winger

career League statistics

Season	Team	Appearances	Goals
2002–2003	Sporting CP	25	3
2003–2004	Manchester United	29	4
2004–2005	Manchester United	33	5
2005–2006	Manchester United	33	9
2006–2007	Manchester United	34	17
2007–2008	Manchester United	34	31
2008–2009	Manchester United	33	18
CAREER		**221**	**87**

achievements

FIFA World Player of the Year: 2008
UEFA Club Footballer of the Year: 2008
Portuguese Footballer of the Year: 2007
FIFPro Special Young Player of the Year:
    2005, 2006
Champions League title with Manchester
    United: 2008
UEFA Team of the Year: 2009

fact Ronaldo's father named him after his favorite
actor, U.S. President Ronald Reagan.

Cristiano Ronaldo

Cristiano Ronaldo is always a huge scoring threat. He's a two-footed attacker, which means the winger can handle and shoot the ball with either foot. Ronaldo takes full advantage of his skills. He can attack from anywhere on the field. The 2008 FIFA World Player of the Year is one of the biggest stars in the game.

Brandon Roy

Brandon Roy quickly made his mark in the NBA. In 2006, he scored 20 points in his first game with the Portland Trail Blazers. Then he scored 19 in his second game. Roy's accurate shooting, passing ability, and good defense quickly made him a star. He won the Rookie of the Year award in 2007. By his second year, he was already an All-Star.

Regular Season Stats

Year	Team	Games	PPG	RPG	APG	SPG
2006–2007	POR	57	16.8	4.4	4.0	1.2
2007–2008	POR	74	19.1	4.7	5.8	1.1
2008–2009	POR	78	22.6	4.7	5.1	1.1
CAREER		**209**	**19.5**	**4.6**	**5.0**	**1.1**

(PPG = points per game; RPG = rebounds per game;
APG = assists per game; SPG = steals per game)

achievements

All-Star selection: 2008, 2009, 2010
Rookie of the Year Award: 2007
Pac-10 Conference Player of the Year: 2006
NCAA All-American: 2006
Scored game-high 18 points at 2008 All-Star Game

fact On January 24, 2009, Roy had 10 steals in one game. His effort set a Portland record.

Name: Johan Alexander Santana
Born: March 13, 1979, in Tovar, Venezuela
Height: 6 feet
Weight: 210 pounds
Bats: Left   Throws: Left
Position: Starting Pitcher

Regular Season Stats

Year	Team	Games	Wins	Losses	Strikeouts	ERA
2000	MIN	30	2	3	64	6.49
2001	MIN	15	1	0	28	4.74
2002	MIN	27	8	6	137	2.99
2003	MIN	45	12	3	169	3.07
2004	MIN	34	20	6	265	2.61
2005	MIN	33	16	7	238	2.87
2006	MIN	34	19	6	245	2.77
2007	MIN	33	15	13	235	3.33
2008	NYM	34	16	7	206	2.53
2009	NYM	25	13	9	146	3.13
CAREER		310	122	60	1,733	3.12

(ERA = earned run average)

achievements

All-Star Game selection: 2005, 2006, 2007, 2009
American League Cy Young Award: 2004, 2006
Gold Glove Award: 2007
Led American League in wins (19) in 2006
Won pitching triple crown in 2006 by leading
    American League in ERA, wins, and strikeouts

fact | Santana started out as a centerfielder.
He was switched to pitching because of
his great arm speed.

Johan Santana

Johan Santana has a blazing fastball and an incredible changeup. His amazing skills have made him one of baseball's best pitchers. Santana started as a relief pitcher for the Minnesota Twins. He soon became a starting pitcher. Santana won the AL Cy Young Award in 2004 and 2006. The lefty was traded to the New York Mets in 2008.

Name: Jose Fernando Torres
Born: March 20, 1984, in Madrid, Spain
Height: 6 feet, 1 inch
Weight: 172 pounds
Position: Striker

Career League Statistics

Season	Team	Appearances	Goals
2000–2001	Atlético Madrid	4	1
2001–2002	Atlético Madrid	36	6
2002–2003	Atlético Madrid	29	13
2003–2004	Atlético Madrid	35	19
2004–2005	Atlético Madrid	38	16
2005–2006	Atlético Madrid	36	13
2006–2007	Atlético Madrid	36	14
2007–2008	Liverpool	33	24
2008–2009	Liverpool	24	14
CAREER		**271**	**120**

achievements

Pro Football Awards Team of the Year: 2008
Top scorer in the UEFA European under-16
    Championship: 2001
Top scorer in the UEFA European under-19
    Championship: 2003
UEFA European Championship Team of the
    Tournament: 2008
Premier League Player of the Month:
    February 2008, September 2009

fact | Torres' nickname is *El Niño*, which is Spanish for "The Kid."

Fernando Torres

Fernando Torres is a real force on the field. He's not afraid to take a shot. And this striker usually gets the goal. Torres first joined Liverpool in the 2007–2008 season. He went on to score 24 goals that year. His powerful shot also made him a hero on Spain's national team. At the Euro 2008 tournament, he scored the game-winning goal to win the championship.

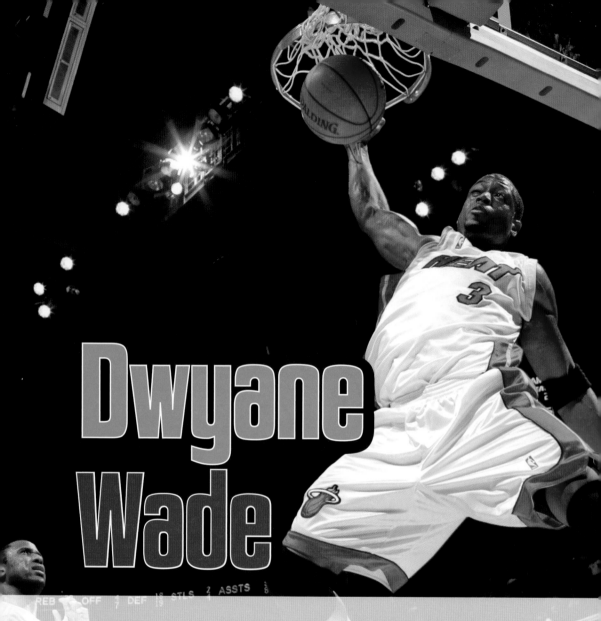

Dwyane Wade

One of Dwyane Wade's nicknames is "Flash." It's no secret why. Wade is lightning-quick with the basketball. He can beat almost any defender off the dribble. He can also slash to the basket or pass to an open teammate. In the 2006 NBA Finals, Wade averaged 34.7 points per game while leading the Miami Heat to the championship.

Name: Dwyane Tyrone Wade
Born: January 17, 1982, in Chicago, Illinois
College: Marquette University
Height: 6 feet, 4 inches
Weight: 216 pounds
Position: Guard

Regular Season Stats

Year	Team	Games	PPG	RPG	APG	SPG
2003–2004	MIA	61	16.2	4.0	4.5	1.4
2004–2005	MIA	77	24.1	5.2	6.8	1.6
2005–2006	MIA	75	27.2	5.7	6.7	1.9
2006–2007	MIA	51	27.4	4.7	7.5	2.1
2007–2008	MIA	51	24.6	4.2	6.9	1.7
2008–2009	MIA	79	30.2	5.0	7.5	2.2
CAREER		**394**	**25.0**	**4.8**	**6.7**	**1.8**

(PPG = points per game; RPG = rebounds per game;
APG = assists per game; SPG = steals per game)

achievements

All-Star selection: 2005, 2006, 2007, 2008, 2009, 2010
NBA champion: 2006
NBA Finals MVP: 2006
All-NBA Second Team: 2005, 2006
Member of U.S. Olympic gold medal team: 2008

fact

In 2003, Wade led the Marquette Golden Eagles to the NCAA's Final Four. He was named a First-Team All-American for his performance.

DeMarcus Ware

Many quarterbacks fear DeMarcus Ware. Since entering the NFL in 2005, the Dallas Cowboys linebacker has been a sack machine. His sack total has increased every season. In 2008, he buried the quarterback a jaw-dropping 20 times! Ware is also an expert at jarring the ball loose. Opposing quarterbacks often fumble the ball when he slams them to the ground.

Full Name: DeMarcus Ware
Born: July 31, 1982, in Auburn, Alabama
College: Troy University
Height: 6 feet, 4 inches
Weight: 262 pounds
Position: Linebacker

Regular Season Defensive Stats

Year	Team	Games	Tackles	Sacks	Int.	FF	TD
2005	DAL	16	47	8.0	0	3	0
2006	DAL	16	59	11.5	1	5	2
2007	DAL	16	60	14.0	0	4	0
2008	DAL	16	69	20.0	0	6	0
2009	DAL	16	45	11.0	0	5	0
CAREER		**80**	**280**	**64.5**	**1**	**23**	**2**

(Int. = interceptions; FF = forced fumbles;
TD = defensive touchdowns)

achievements

Pro Bowl selection: 2006, 2007, 2008, 2009
First-Team All-Pro selection: 2007, 2008, 2009
NFL sack leader (20) in 2008
Butkus Award winner as NFL's best
    linebacker: 2008
Sun Belt Conference Defensive Player
    of the Year: 2004

fact | In 2008, Ware tied an NFL record by getting at least one sack for 10 straight games.

personal information

Name: Shaun Roger White
Born: September 3, 1986, in
San Diego, California
Height: 5 feet, 8 inches
Weight: 141 pounds
Stance: Regular
Sports: Snowboarding, Skateboarding

career Snowboarding Titles

Year	X Games	Olympics	Dew Tour
2002	2	0	--
2003	2	--	--
2004	1	--	--
2005	1	--	--
2006	2	1	--
2007	2	--	--
2008	2	--	2
2009	2	--	4
2010	1	1	--
CAREER	**15**	**2**	**6**

achievements

Won gold at the 2007 X Games in
vert skateboarding
Transworld Snowboarding Rider of the Year:
2003, 2006
Has won a record 16 combined gold medals at
X Games and Winter X Games
Olympic Gold Medal, Halfpipe: 2006, 2010

fact Shaun White is also a world-class
skateboarder. He won the skateboard
vert event at the 2007 X Games.

Shaun White

Snowboarder Shaun White has certainly earned his nickname, "The Flying Tomato." He sails through the air with his long, bright red hair flowing behind him. White is a master of the halfpipe. He wows crowds with signature moves like the Double McTwist 1260. His high-flying stunts helped him win gold at the 2006 and 2010 Winter Olympics.

Index

Sports Illustrated KIDS Greatest Sports Stars is published by Capstone Press,
151 Good Counsel Drive, P.O. Box 669, Mankato, Minnesota 56002.
www.capstonepub.com

Printed in the United States of America in North Mankato, Minnesota.

042010
005763R

Library of Congress Cataloging-in-Publication Data
Doeden, Matt.
    Sports illustrated kids greatest sports stars / by Matt Doeden.
    p. cm.—(Sports illustrated kids)
    Includes bibliographical references and index.
    ISBN 978-1-4296-5035-9 (paperback)
    1. Athletes—United States—Biography. I. Title. II. Series.
GV697.A1D63 2010
796.0922—dc22
[B]   2010007247

Editorial Credits
Aaron Sautter, editor; Tracy Davies and Gene Bentdahl, designers;
    Eric Gohl, media researcher; Blake Hoena, production specialist

Photo Credits
Corbis/EPA/Alberto Martin, cover (top right)
Dreamstime/Santamaradona, 3 (center left); Szirtesi, 7 (right)
Getty Images Inc./Kevork Djansezian, 103; Simon Bruty, 97
MLB Photos via Getty Images/Mark Cunningham, 56
Sports Illustrated/Al Tielemans, 2 (right), 3 (bottom middle), 36, 86; Bill Frakes, 12, 17, 42;
    Bob Martin, 9 (top right), 54, 70, 109; Bob Rosato, 8 (top left & bottom), 19, 24, 52,
    58, 64, 73, 94, 104; Chuck Solomon, 3 (top left), 40, 91, 92; Damian Strohmeyer, 6–7
    (background), 6 (left), 8 (top right), 9 (top left), 15, 20, 34, 38, 63, 68, 75, 101; David
    E. Klutho, cover (top left & bottom left), 2 (left), 6 (right), 23, 27, 47, 51, 88; Heinz
    Kluetmeier, 9 (center right), 85; John Biever, 2 (middle), 3 (bottom right), 61, 106; John
    Iacono, 44, 49; John W. McDonough, cover (bottom right), 3 (top middle), 7 (left), 8
    (center right), 11, 30, 67, 79, 81, 83, 98; Manny Millan, 9 (bottom left); Peter Read Miller,
    32; Robert Beck, cover (top middle), 3 (top right & center right), 8 (center left), 9 (center
    left), 76; Simon Bruty, 3 (bottom left), 9 (bottom right), 28

Statistics in this book are current through the 2008–2009 season.